LOW-FAT
COOKBOOK

Delicious healthy eating for all the family

CONTENTS

Guide to symbols

The recipes in this book are accompanied by symbols that alert you to important information.

 Tells you how many people the recipe serves, or how much is produced.

 Indicates how much time you will need to prepare and cook a dish. Next to this symbol you will also find out if additional time is required for such things as marinating, standing, proving, or cooling. You need to read the recipe to find out exactly how much extra time is needed.

 Alerts you to what has to be done before you can begin to cook the recipe, or to parts of the recipe that take a long time to complete.

 Denotes that special equipment is required. Where possible, alternatives are given.

 Accompanies freezing information.

Egg noodles with lemon and herbs

Fresh Asian noodles absorb the flavours they are cooked in.

INGREDIENTS

2 tbsp vegetable oil

4 spring onions, finely sliced,
   plus 1 extra,
   finely shredded, to garnish

1 lemongrass stalk, very finely sliced

2.5cm (1in) piece of fresh root ginger,
   peeled and grated

350g (12oz) fresh egg noodles
   or 175g (6oz) dried egg noodles,
   cooked

2 tbsp light soy sauce

juice of 1 lemon

pinch of sugar

2 tbsp snipped chives

2 tbsp chopped flat-leaf parsley

lemon zest, cut into fine
   strips, to garnish

METHOD

1 Heat the oil in a wok or large, deep frying pan, add the spring onions, lemongrass, and ginger, and stir-fry for 1 minute.

2 Add the noodles and toss over the heat for 2 minutes. Mix together the soy sauce, lemon juice, and sugar, and pour over the noodles. Stir-fry for a further 2 minutes, or until the noodles are heated through.

3 Sprinkle the chives and parsley over the top, then toss with the noodles and transfer to a serving bowl. Serve at once, garnished with the lemon zest and spring onion.

serves 4

prep 10 mins
• cook 5 mins

Vegetable Pad Thai

This popular Thai noodle dish is made more substantial by adding tofu.

INGREDIENTS

250g (9oz) wide or medium
  rice noodles
2–3 tbsp vegetable oil
200g (7oz) firm tofu, cut into cubes
2 garlic cloves, grated or
  finely chopped
1 egg, lightly beaten
150ml (5fl oz) hot vegetable stock
juice of 1 lime
1 tsp Thai fish sauce, such as
  nam pla (optional)

2 tsp tamarind paste
2 tsp demerara sugar
1 tbsp dark soy sauce
1 red chilli, deseeded and
  finely chopped
25g (scant 1 oz) dry-roasted peanuts,
  roughly chopped
1 bunch of spring onions, finely chopped
75g (2½oz) beansprouts (optional)
small handful of coriander
  leaves, to serve

METHOD

1 Soak the rice noodles in boiling water for 10 minutes, then drain. Meanwhile, heat 1 tablespoon of the vegetable oil in a wok over a medium-high heat, and swirl it around to coat the surface. Add the tofu, and cook for about 10 minutes until golden. Remove with a slotted spoon, and set aside.

2 Add another tablespoon of oil to the pan. When hot, add the garlic and cook for 10 seconds, then tip in the egg and cook, stirring and breaking it up with a wooden spoon, until scrambled. Remove from the pan, and set aside.

3 Add half a tablespoon of the oil. When hot, add the drained noodles, and stir gently to coat with the oil. Pour over the stock, lime juice, fish sauce if using, tamarind paste, sugar, and soy sauce; toss to combine. Let it simmer for a few minutes, sprinkle over the chilli, and stir through.

4 Add half of the peanuts, the spring onions, and the beansprouts (if using), and stir-fry for a minute. Now add the reserved tofu and scrambled egg, stir to combine, and transfer to a serving plate. Scatter over the remaining peanuts and a sprinkling of coriander leaves to serve.

serves 4

prep 15 mins
• cook 15 mins

wok

Pasta with hot pepper sauce

Keep oil and cheese to a minimum, and pasta can be an ideal everyday low-fat food.

INGREDIENTS

1 tbsp olive oil
1 onion, finely chopped
salt and freshly ground black pepper
2 garlic cloves, grated or
   finely chopped
2 red chillies, deseeded and
   finely chopped
2 red peppers and 1 yellow pepper,
   deseeded and roughly chopped
350g (12oz) penne or large
   pasta shells
handful of basil leaves, torn
15g (½oz) Parmesan cheese, grated
good-quality thick balsamic
   vinegar (optional)

METHOD

1 Heat the oil in a large frying pan, add the onion, and cook on a low heat for 5 minutes, or until soft and translucent. Season well with salt and pepper. Add the garlic and chillies and cook for a few seconds more. Add the peppers and cook, stirring occasionally, on a low heat for 5 minutes, or until soft.
2 Meanwhile, cook the pasta in a pan of boiling salted water for 8 minutes, or until it is cooked but still firm to the bite. Drain, keeping back a tiny amount of the cooking water. Return the pasta to the pan and toss together. Add the pepper mixture and the basil and toss well. Sprinkle with Parmesan and balsamic vinegar (if using), and serve.

serves 4

prep 10 mins
• cook 15 mins

Lemony dahl

In India, this is known as *masoor dahl*, and can feature as part of any meal.

INGREDIENTS
1 tbsp olive oil
1 onion, finely chopped
salt and freshly ground black pepper
2 garlic cloves, grated or finely chopped
5cm (2in) piece of fresh root
  ginger, grated
pinch of ground turmeric
pinch of garam masala
300g (10oz) red lentils
grated zest and juice of 1 lemon
900ml (1½ pints) hot vegetable stock
2 tomatoes, skinned and chopped
handful of coriander leaves,
  finely chopped

METHOD
1 Heat the oil in a saucepan over a low heat. Add the onion and a pinch of salt, and sweat for 5 minutes until soft and translucent. Stir in the garlic, ginger, turmeric, and garam masala, and cook for 1 minute.
2 Stir in the lentils and lemon zest, pour over the stock, and simmer for about 20 minutes, or until the lentils are cooked.
3 Season well with salt and pepper, and stir through the lemon juice, tomatoes, and coriander leaves. Serve hot with naan bread or chapatis.

serves 4

prep 10 mins
• cook 30 mins

Potato and pea curry

This dish is found on dining tables all over India.

INGREDIENTS
1 tbsp sunflower oil
2.5cm (1in) piece of fresh root ginger,
  peeled and finely chopped
2–3 green chillies, deseeded and
  finely chopped
1 tsp cumin seeds
1 tsp mustard seeds
small handful of curry leaves
6 tomatoes, skinned and chopped
675g (1½lb) waxy potatoes,
  peeled and cubed
1 tsp ground turmeric
300ml (10fl oz) hot vegetable stock
75g (2½oz) frozen peas
salt and freshly ground black pepper
handful of coriander leaves,
  finely chopped

METHOD
1 Heat the oil in a large frying pan over a medium heat. Add the ginger, chillies, cumin
   seeds, and mustard seeds, and crumble in the curry leaves. Cook for a couple of minutes
   until the mustard seeds start to pop. Add the tomatoes, stir through, and cook for a few
   more minutes.
2 Add the potatoes and turmeric, and pour in the stock. Bring to the boil, reduce the heat
   slightly, cover, and simmer for about 15 minutes.
3 Tip in the peas, stir through, and cook for a further 5–10 minutes. Season well with salt
   and pepper, and stir through the coriander. Serve hot with rice or naan bread.

serves 4   prep 10 mins
               • cook 30 mins

Cabbage rolls

Derived from a German recipe, stuffed cabbage leaves in tomato sauce make a delicious supper dish.

INGREDIENTS

1 tbsp oil, plus extra for greasing
1 leek, white part only, finely chopped
115g (4oz) chanterelle mushrooms, finely chopped
1 celery stick, finely chopped
115g (4oz) fresh brown breadcrumbs
1 egg, lightly beaten
2 tbsp chopped flat-leaf parsley
pinch of ground coriander
1 tbsp lemon juice

sea salt and freshly ground black pepper
8 large Savoy cabbage leaves or winter cabbage leaves, stalks removed
150ml (5fl oz) vegetable stock

For the sauce

1 tbsp olive oil
1 onion, finely chopped
2 garlic cloves, crushed
400g carton passata
salt and freshly ground black pepper

METHOD

1 Heat the oil in a frying pan and fry the leek, mushrooms, and celery over a low heat for 5 minutes, or until soft. Remove from the heat. Stir in the breadcrumbs, egg, parsley, coriander, and lemon juice, and season with salt and pepper. Set aside until needed.

2 Preheat the oven to 160°C (325°F/Gas 3). Blanch the cabbage leaves in boiling salted water for 2 minutes, then rinse in cold water, and drain well.

3 Lay the leaves flat and divide the stuffing among them. Roll up each leaf, folding in the sides to make a neat parcel. Pack the rolls tightly in an oiled ovenproof dish, pour in the vegetable stock, and bake for 45–55 minutes, or until tender.

4 Meanwhile, make the tomato sauce. Heat oil in the frying pan over a medium heat, and fry the onion and garlic, stirring frequently, for 4–5 minutes, or until soft. Add the passata, and cook on a low heat, stirring occasionally, for 10 minutes. Season with salt and pepper.

5 Remove the rolls from the oven and lift them out of the dish using a slotted spoon. Discard the stock. Spoon some of the tomato sauce on to serving plates and place the cabbage rolls on top. Serve immediately, with the remaining sauce served separately.

serves 4

prep 30 mins
• cook 1 hour 20 mins

Bean burgers

A tasty and low-fat alternative to burgers made with meat.

INGREDIENTS

400g can aduki beans, drained
   and rinsed
400g can chickpeas, drained
   and rinsed
1 onion, roughly chopped
6 salted anchovies in olive oil,
   drained
1 tbsp wholegrain mustard
salt and freshly ground black pepper
2 eggs
2–3 tbsp plain flour, plus
   extra for dusting
2–3 tbsp vegetable or sunflower
   oil, for frying

METHOD

1 Put the drained beans and chickpeas in a food processor, and pulse several times until
   the beans are broken up.
2 Add the onion, anchovies, and mustard to the food processor, and season well with salt
   and pepper. Pulse again a few times. You want the mixture to be well combined, but not
   sloppy. Now add the eggs, and pulse again until combined. Add the flour (just enough to
   bind the burgers), and pulse until incorporated.
3 Heat 1 tablespoon of oil in a large non-stick frying pan over a medium heat. Once the oil
   is hot, spoon out a portion of the bean mixture (it makes 6 burgers) and, using lots of
   flour on your hands, form into a flattened burger before adding to the pan.
   Fry undisturbed for 2–3 minutes on each side until firm and golden. Cook in batches of
   2 or 3 burgers at a time, forming the burgers as you go and adding more oil when needed.
   Serve hot, sandwiched in a bun with crisp lettuce and tomato ketchup.

serves 6   prep 15 mins   food processor
                  • cook 10 mins

Courgette and pea mini tortillas

A perfect choice for entertaining, tortillas can be made with all sorts of fillings.

INGREDIENTS

500g (1lb 2oz) courgettes, grated
50g (1¾oz) baby spinach leaves
grated zest and juice of 1 lemon
250g (9oz) frozen peas, thawed
25g (scant 1oz) pine nuts, toasted
salt and freshly ground black pepper
10 wheat tortillas, halved
2 tbsp reduced-fat mayonnaise
mangetout (snow pea) sprouts
  and pea shoots

METHOD

1 In a large bowl, mix together the grated courgettes, spinach, lemon zest and juice, peas, and pine nuts. Season with salt and pepper.
2 Heat a dry frying pan over a high heat. Add the tortilla halves, 2 at a time, and toast for about 15 seconds on each side. As you cook, set aside the tortilla halves under a clean tea towel to keep warm.
3 Lay one of the tortilla halves flat on a chopping board, and brush lightly with the mayonnaise. Take some of the filling, and place in the centre. Arrange some of the mangetout sprouts and pea shoots on top, so that they stick out at one end, then gently roll up the mini tortilla. Repeat this process until you have made 20 mini tortillas in all.
4 To serve, arrange the mini tortillas on individual serving plates, allowing 2 per person.

serves 10

prep 20 mins
• cook 5 mins

Vegetarian moussaka

A healthier, but equally delicious, take on this famous Greek dish.

INGREDIENTS
1 tbsp olive oil
1 onion, finely chopped
salt and freshly ground black pepper
1 tsp dried mint
3 tsp dried oregano
400g can aduki beans,
   drained and rinsed
700g jar passata
25g (scant 1oz) pine nuts
250ml (9fl oz) 2 per cent fat,
   Greek-style yogurt
1 egg, lightly beaten

METHOD
1 Preheat the oven to 200°C (400°F/Gas 6). Heat the oil in a saucepan over a low heat. Add the onion and a pinch of salt, and sweat gently for about 5 minutes until soft. Sprinkle over the dried mint and 1 teaspoon of the dried oregano, and stir through.
2 Add the aduki beans, passata, and pine nuts, and bring to the boil. Reduce the heat to low, and simmer gently for 15–20 minutes until thickened. Season well with salt and pepper.
3 Spoon the bean mixture into an ovenproof dish. Mix together the yogurt, egg, and remaining 2 teaspoons of dried oregano. Spoon evenly over the top of the bean mixture. Bake in the oven for 15–20 minutes, until the top is golden, puffed, and set. Serve hot with a crisp green salad.

serves 4

prep 15 mins
• cook 45 mins

Jamaican-style fish with sweet potatoes

Strong Caribbean spices are beautifully offset by sweet potatoes and succulent fish.

INGREDIENTS

1 tsp allspice
1 tsp paprika
5cm (2in) piece of fresh root ginger,
   peeled and finely sliced
2 red chillies, deseeded and
   finely chopped
1 tbsp olive oil
salt and freshly ground black pepper
4 fillets of white fish, such as
   haddock or cod,
   about 200g (7oz) each
4 sweet potatoes, peeled and cut
   into bite-sized pieces
handful of coriander, finely chopped

METHOD

1 Preheat the oven to 190°C (375°F/Gas 5). Mix the allspice, paprika, ginger, and chillies with the olive oil. Add a pinch of salt and lots of black pepper. Smother the fish with most of the spice mixture. Put to one side. Toss the sweet potatoes with the remaining spice mixture and place in a roasting tin. Put in the oven to roast for 15 minutes.

2 Add the fish to the roasting tin and roast for 15 minutes, or until the sweet potatoes and fish are cooked. Sprinkle with coriander and serve.

serves 4

prep 15 mins
• cook 30 mins

Teriyaki fish with noodles

Delicately flavoured white fish provides a perfect platform for this classic Japanese marinade.

INGREDIENTS

4 cod loins, about 150g (5½oz) each
250g (9oz) thick or medium udon
   noodles
4 spring onions, sliced
handful of coriander, leaves only
lime quarters, to serve

For the teriyaki sauce

1–2 tbsp dark soy sauce
1 tbsp clear honey
2.5cm (1in) piece of fresh root ginger,
   peeled and grated
pinch of sugar
1 tbsp mirin or dry sherry

METHOD

1 Preheat the oven to 200°C (400°F/Gas 6). To make the teriyaki sauce, put all the ingredients in a bowl, and mix well. Pour the sauce over the fish, and leave to marinate for about 10 minutes.
2 Sit the fish pieces with the sauce in a roasting tin, and bake in the oven for about 15 minutes, or until the fish is cooked through.
3 Meanwhile, put the noodles in a bowl, and pour over boiling water. Leave for few minutes until soft, then drain and toss with the spring onions and coriander. Serve with the fish and lime quarters.

serves 4

prep 10 mins
plus marinating
• cook 15 mins

Roasted monkfish with chilli, tomatoes, anchovies, and capers

The delicate flavour of monkfish is delicious with spicy chillies, salty anchovies, and fresh tomatoes.

INGREDIENTS
1kg (2¼lb) monkfish tail fillets
drizzle of olive oil
salt and freshly ground black pepper
2 red chillies, deseeded and
  very finely chopped
6–8 salted anchovies, finely chopped
2–3 tsp capers, rinsed, drained,
  and chopped
12 cherry tomatoes

METHOD
1 Preheat the oven to 200°C (400°F/Gas 6). Sit the monkfish fillets in a roasting tin, and drizzle over a little olive oil. Season well with salt and pepper, and set aside.
2 Using a mortar and pestle, pound together the chillies, anchovies, and capers until they become a paste. Alternatively, mash into a paste with a fork. Using your hands, smother the monkfish with the paste.
3 Put the fish in a roasting tin, and cook in the oven for about 10 minutes. Remove the tin from the oven, add the tomatoes, and roast for a further 5–10 minutes, or until the fish is cooked through.
4 Leave to rest for 5 minutes, then slice and serve immediately with either a green salad or baby roast potatoes.

serves 4

prep 20 mins
• cook 20 mins

Pan-fried prawns, olives, and tomatoes

A sunny burst of Spanish flavours make this a delicious summer dish.

INGREDIENTS

1 tbsp olive oil
1 onion, finely chopped
2 garlic cloves, grated or finely
   chopped
12 large raw prawns, peeled and
   deveined, but with tail left intact
splash of dry sherry
6 tomatoes, skinned
large handful of mixed olives, pitted
handful of basil, chopped
handful of flat-leaf
   parsley, chopped
salt and freshly ground black pepper

METHOD

1 Heat the oil in a large frying pan over a medium heat. Add the onion, and sauté for about 5 minutes until soft and translucent. Add the garlic, and cook for a few seconds, then add the prawns and cook over a high heat until the prawns are just turning pink.
2 Add the sherry, and continue cooking for 5 minutes, stirring, until the alcohol has evaporated. Add the tomatoes and olives and cook for a further 1–2 minutes, stirring occasionally, until the tomatoes start to break down. Stir through the herbs, and season well with salt and pepper. Serve immediately with fresh crusty bread.

serves 4

prep 5 mins
• cook 15 mins

Roast chicken with thyme and lemon

Lemon and thyme are traditional accompaniments to chicken. Here they are combined with butter to make a simple, yet delicious, glaze.

INGREDIENTS

1.8kg (4lb) chicken, jointed into 8 pieces
1 lemon
2 garlic cloves, crushed
15g (½oz) butter, softened
1 tbsp olive oil
1 small bunch of thyme,
   leaves removed from stalks
salt and freshly ground black pepper
120ml (4fl oz) dry white wine

METHOD

1 Preheat the oven to 200°C (400°F/Gas 6). Place the chicken pieces in the roasting tin, in one layer.
2 Finely grate 2 teaspoons of zest from the lemon, reserving the lemon. Place the zest in a bowl with the garlic, butter, oil, and thyme leaves, and season to taste with salt and pepper. Beat with a wooden spoon to mix.
3 Dot the butter mixture evenly over the chicken pieces. Cut the reserved lemon into chunks and tuck around the chicken, then pour over the wine.
4 Roast the chicken, turning and basting the chicken pieces occasionally, for 50–60 minutes, or until the chicken is golden brown and cooked through and the juices run clear when the meat is pierced with a knife. Add a little more wine if the juices start to boil dry.
5 Once cooked, allow to rest for 10 minutes. Remove the chicken skins and discard them, then serve.

serves 4

prep 5 mins
plus resting
• cook 1 hour

Chicken biryani

For special occasions, this subtly spiced, aromatic dish from India is traditionally decorated with pieces of edible silver leaf.

INGREDIENTS

2 tbsp vegetable oil

15g (½oz) butter or ghee

1 large onion, thinly sliced

2 garlic cloves, crushed

6 curry leaves

6 cardamom pods

1 cinnamon stick, broken into 2 or 3 pieces

1 tsp ground turmeric

½ tsp ground cumin

4 skinless, boneless chicken breasts, cut into 2.5cm (1in) pieces

3 tbsp mild curry paste

300g (10oz) basmati rice

85g (3oz) sultanas

900ml (1½ pints) chicken stock

2 tbsp flaked almonds, toasted

METHOD

1 Heat the oil and butter or ghee in a large, deep saucepan, and gently fry the onion and garlic until softened and starting to turn golden. Add the curry leaves, cardamom pods, and cinnamon stick, and fry for 5 minutes, stirring occasionally.

2 Add the turmeric and cumin, fry for 1 minute, then add the chicken, and stir in the curry paste.

3 Add the rice and sultanas, stir well, then pour in enough of the stock to cover the rice. Bring to the boil, lower the heat, and cook gently for 10–12 minutes, or until the rice is cooked, adding more stock if the mixture becomes dry.

4 Transfer to a serving dish, fluff up the rice with a fork, and serve with flaked almonds scattered over the top.

serves 4

prep 20 mins
• cook 30 mins

Chicken pinwheels with pasta

These little rolls of chicken breast are packed with Mediterranean flavours.

INGREDIENTS

4 skinless, boneless chicken breasts
salt and freshly ground black pepper
1 garlic clove, crushed
25g (scant 1oz) basil leaves, plus
  extra to garnish
115g (4oz) sun-dried tomatoes
  in oil, drained
1 tbsp olive oil, plus extra for brushing
200ml (7fl oz) passata
200ml (7fl oz) dry white wine
cooked pasta, to serve

METHOD

1 Preheat the oven to 200°C (400°F/Gas 6). Lay the chicken breasts on a board between 2 sheets of cling film and beat flat with a rolling pin to 5mm (¼in) thick.

2 Season the chicken with salt and pepper then spread with the garlic. Arrange the basil leaves and sun-dried tomatoes evenly over the surface of the chicken.

3 Roll up the chicken from the shorter sides to enclose the filling, forming a firm roll. Secure with fine string or wooden cocktail sticks. Heat the oil in a frying pan and brown the chicken rolls on all sides. Transfer to a shallow ovenproof dish. Brush with a little oil and bake for 20–25 minutes.

4 Put the passata and wine in a saucepan and simmer gently for 10 minutes, or until thickened slightly. When the chicken is cooked, remove from the dish and pour any juices into the passata.

5 Cut the chicken into neat slices. Arrange the slices on individual serving plates and serve with the pasta and sauce on the side. Garnish with basil.

serves 4

prep 20 mins
• cook 40 mins

fine string
or wooden
cocktail sticks

freeze the
pinwheels for
1 month

Spiced turkey and greens stir-fry

Add some Asian inspiration to leftover turkey.

INGREDIENTS

350g (12oz) cooked turkey, skin
  removed, roughly chopped
2 heads of Asian greens such as pak choi,
  trimmed and roughly chopped
1 tbsp sunflower oil
1 onion, finely chopped
5cm (2in) piece of fresh root ginger,
  peeled and finely sliced
3 garlic cloves, grated or finely chopped
2 green chillies, deseeded and finely
  chopped
1 tbsp dark soy sauce
1 tbsp mirin
handful of basil leaves, torn
salt and freshly ground black pepper

METHOD

1 Put the cooked turkey in a food processor, and process until minced; be careful not to turn it into a paste. Cook the greens in a pan of boiling salted water for about 5 minutes until just wilted. Drain, and set aside.
2 Heat the oil in a wok or large frying pan over a low heat. Add the onion, and sweat gently for about 5 minutes until soft and translucent. Add the ginger, garlic, and chillies, and cook for a further 5 minutes, stirring constantly.
3 Tip in the minced turkey, and stir well to combine. Add the soy sauce and mirin, and stir-fry for 5–8 minutes until the turkey is warmed through. Stir through the reserved greens and the basil, and season with salt and pepper. Serve immediately.

serves 4

prep 10 mins
• cook 25 mins

food processor

Asian turkey and noodle soup

A light, fragrant, and restorative broth.

INGREDIENTS

900ml (1½ pints) vegetable stock
2 tbsp soy sauce
1 lemongrass stalk, sliced
2.5cm (1in) piece of fresh root ginger,
   peeled and sliced
2 skinless turkey breast fillets, about
   400g (14oz) each
300g (10oz) fine rice noodles
1 red chilli, deseeded and sliced
handful of coriander leaves
salt

METHOD

1 Heat the vegetable stock in a large saucepan over a medium heat. Once hot, add the
   soy sauce, lemongrass, ginger, and turkey breast fillets. Bring to the boil, reduce the heat
   slightly, and simmer for 15–20 minutes until the turkey is cooked through. Remove the
   turkey fillets with a slotted spoon and set aside to cool.
2 To cook the noodles, bring the poaching liquid to the boil, topping up with boiling
   water if needed. Add the rice noodles and chilli, reduce the heat slightly, and simmer for
   1 minute. Shred the turkey and return it to the pan, with the coriander leaves, to heat
   through. Season with salt to taste, and serve immediately.

serves 4

prep 10 mins
plus cooling
• cook 30 mins

Pork steaks with tomato and broad bean sauce

Plenty of flavour is packed into this tomato and herb sauce.

INGREDIENTS
4 pork steaks, about 150g (5½oz)
   each, trimmed
2 tbsp olive oil
pinch of dried oregano
salt and freshly ground black pepper
1 onion, finely chopped
2 garlic cloves, grated or finely chopped
400g can whole peeled plum
   tomatoes, chopped
125g (4½oz) frozen broad beans,
   or use fresh if in season
handful of flat-leaf parsley,
   very finely chopped

METHOD
1 Preheat the oven to 200°C (400°F/Gas 6). Brush the steaks with 1 tablespoon of the oil, and sprinkle over the oregano. Season well with salt and pepper. Place the steaks in a roasting tin, and roast in the oven for 15 minutes until golden and cooked through.
2 Meanwhile, make the sauce. Heat the remaining oil in a frying pan over a low heat, and add the onion and a pinch of salt. Sweat for 5 minutes until soft and translucent, then add the garlic and stir for a couple of seconds.
3 Add the tomatoes, including any juices, and bring to the boil. Reduce the heat slightly, and simmer for about 15 minutes. Add the broad beans, and cook for a further 10 minutes, adding a little water if the mixture dries out.
4 When ready to serve, taste the sauce, and season if needed. Stir through the parsley. Spoon the sauce on to plates, sit the steaks on the sauce, and serve hot.

serves 4

prep 10 mins
• cook 30 mins

Chinese chilli beef stir-fry

This Chinese stir-fry is a good choice for those who like their dishes spicy rather than sweet and sour.

INGREDIENTS

500g (1lb 2oz) rump steak,
   cut into thin strips
3 tbsp dark soy sauce
2 tbsp rice vinegar
1 tbsp ground Chinese five-spice
freshly ground black pepper
2 tbsp vegetable oil
1 large red chilli, deseeded
   and finely chopped
1 garlic clove, crushed

1 tsp fresh root ginger, peeled
   and grated
½ red pepper, deseeded and thinly sliced
100g (3½oz) mangetout, halved lengthways
100g (3½oz) tenderstem broccoli
1 tsp cornflour
120ml (4fl oz) beef stock
few drops of toasted sesame oil

METHOD

1 Put the beef strips in a bowl with the soy sauce, rice vinegar, and five-spice powder, stirring until coated. Season with black pepper, cover the bowl with cling film, and leave to marinate for several hours, or overnight in the refrigerator.

2 Heat 1 tablespoon of the oil in a wok, add the chilli, garlic, ginger, and red pepper, and stir-fry for 3 minutes. Add the mangetout and broccoli, and stir-fry for 2 minutes. Remove the vegetables and set aside.

3 Add the rest of the oil, remove the beef from the marinade using a slotted spoon (reserving the marinade), and stir-fry over a high heat for 1 minute. Return the vegetables to the wok, and add the marinade. Stir the cornflour into the stock and gradually pour the mixture into the wok. Bring to the boil, stirring, for 1–2 minutes, or until piping hot.

4 Drizzle over the sesame oil, and serve at once with boiled rice or egg noodles.

serves 4

prep 15 mins
plus marinating
• cook 10 mins

wok

marinate for several
hours, or overnight
if possible

Beef with beetroot and spinach

This handy dish is quick to make and offers a wonderful variety of flavours and textures.

INGREDIENTS

350g (12oz) cooked beef, sliced
250g (9oz) fresh spinach leaves, rinsed
450g (1lb) ready-cooked beetroot, not in
 vinegar, quartered
2 tbsp extra virgin olive oil
1 tbsp balsamic vinegar
juice of ½ clementine or satsuma
salt and freshly ground black pepper
handful of thyme, leaves picked

METHOD

1 In a large bowl, gently toss together the cooked beef, spinach, and beetroot. In a small bowl or jug, whisk together the olive oil, balsamic vinegar, and citrus juice. Season with salt and pepper.
2 When ready to serve, drizzle the dressing over the beef and beetroot salad, and scatter over the thyme leaves.

serves 4

prep 15 mins

Lamb kebabs

The simple marinade helps tenderize the meat, as well as imparting flavour.

INGREDIENTS
450g (1lb) boned leg, fillet, or shoulder of
   lamb, cut into 2.5cm (1in) cubes
salt and freshly ground black pepper
16 shallots, blanched and peeled
16 cherry tomatoes
16 button mushrooms
1 red pepper, deseeded and cut into
   square pieces
pitta bread, to serve
salad leaves, to serve

For the marinade
1 tbsp olive oil
juice of 1 lemon
1 small red onion, finely chopped
1 tbsp lemon thyme leaves

METHOD
1 Mix the marinade ingredients in a large bowl. Add the lamb pieces, stir well to coat in the marinade, then season with salt and pepper. Cover, and chill for 2 hours, stirring occasionally. Soak the wooden skewers in cold water.
2 Preheat the grill to medium. Assemble the kebabs by threading the meat and prepared vegetables on to the skewers. Grill for 10–15 minutes, turning frequently.
3 Serve at once, with warmed pitta bread and salad leaves.

serves 4

**prep 15 mins
plus marinating
cook 10-15 mins**

**8 wooden
skewers**

**marinate for 2 hrs
• soak the skewers
for at least 30 mins
before using, to
prevent burning**

London, New York, Melbourne, Munich, and Delhi

Editor Cécile Landau

Jacket Designer Mark Penfound

DTP Designer Kavita Varma

DK INDIA

Editorial Consultant Dipali Singh

Designer Neha Ahuja

DTP Designer Tarun Sharma

DTP Coordinator Sunil Sharma

Head of Publishing Aparna Sharma

First published in Great Britain in 2013.
Material in this publication was previously published
in *The Cooking Book* (2008) , and *Cook Express* (2009)
by Dorling Kindersley Limited
80 Strand, London WC2R oRL
Penguin Group (UK)

10 9 8 7 6 5 4 3 2 1
001-192531-Feb/13

A CIP catalogue record for this book is available
from the British Library.

ISBN 978-1-4093-2596-3

Printed and bound in China by Hung Hing Printing Co. Ltd.